AF119034

YOUR KNOWLEDGE HAS VALUE

- We will publish your bachelor's and
  master's thesis, essays and papers

- Your own eBook and book -
  sold worldwide in all relevant shops

- Earn money with each sale

Upload your text at www.GRIN.com
and publish for free

Dessalegn Oulte

Multi-ethnicity and Development

GRIN Publishing

Bibliographic information published by the German National Library:

The German National Library lists this publication in the National Bibliography; detailed bibliographic data are available on the Internet at http://dnb.dnb.de .

Imprint:

Copyright © 2011 GRIN Verlag, Open Publishing GmbH
Print and binding: Books on Demand GmbH, Norderstedt Germany
ISBN: 978-3-640-90340-5

This book at GRIN:

http://www.grin.com/en/e-book/170855/multi-ethnicity-and-development

GRIN - Your knowledge has value

Since its foundation in 1998, GRIN has specialized in publishing academic texts by students, college teachers and other academics as e-book and printed book. The website www.grin.com is an ideal platform for presenting term papers, final papers, scientific essays, dissertations and specialist books.

Visit us on the internet:

http://www.grin.com/

http://www.facebook.com/grincom

http://www.twitter.com/grin_com

MULTI-ETHNICITY AND DEVELOPMENT

A Term Paper

Mekele University, Institute Of Pale Environment and Heritage Conservation

February 2011

CONTENT

1. **Introduction: Multi ethnicity and development**

Ethnicity is fundamental issue in human life as 90 percent the world's nations are composed of two or more ethnic groups. The action-reaction relationship existed between dominant group and minority groups often negatively affected many nations' development in different social, political economical perspective. Ethnic background of certain population determines cooperative or non-cooperative results of communication as it has been evidently seen that majority of world conflicts are a result of, or related to ethnic issues. Factors eliciting conflict such as collective disadvantage ,lose of political economy and repressions are aspects of ethnicity (Hailemariam, 2010).

2. **Advantages and disadvantages of multi -ethnicity**

The existence of two or more ethnic groups in a given society may characterized by peace full co existence and harmony, or conflict and violence. Based on this fact the attitude of people about the advantages and disadvantages of multi ethnicity is also having two categories. Some agree that ethnic society have some useful aspect in maintaining warm relationship among diverse groups, motivating people to exchange visits, and help each other (as some ethnic groups organized to do so) (peterI.Rose,penina M.Glazer,Myron glazer, 1978). There are certain national states in which multipile cultural groups live together in reasonable harmony. Multyi ethnic countries like Switzerland , Indonesia and Madagascar maintained the peaceful co-existance of multyi ethnic groups in harmoyny, with no domination of one group by the other.Switzerland could be a model country in achieving these advantages by allowing each groups to maintain its identity, language and culture. In Madagascar, linguistic and cultural similarity facilitated such harmony. Uniform educational system inherited from French colonial rule also contributed to national unity. In Indonesia common language and colonial school system promoted ethnic harmony, national identity and integration (Anderson,1991 cited in (Kottak, 2002).

By observing such kind of harmony in certain nations, some argue that the existence of different ethnic groups could not be a cause   for the eruption of conflict in a given society. According to these arguments, in many places of around the world, ethnic and racial groups live together in comparative harmony so that political, social or economic factors are primary causes rather than ethnic identity (John and Erna perry, 1976:pp 230).

Social scientists discovered that ethnic harmony could be best achieved and personal contact among members of different racial and ethnic groups is most likely to reduce prejudice if :

- The individuals are equal in status
- Their interaction has the support of a legitimate authority such as the government
- They are emotionally involved in the interaction

- They gain social rewards such as prestige, or power from the experience and
- The members of different groups are inter dependent

Contact is unlike to reduce prejudice if the members of the different groups are unequal status .completion rather than cooperation can increase prejudice. Tension during the social interaction and fear that one group will lose prestige or power can also increase prejudice (Amir, 1969 cited in E.Conklin, 1987).

Another perspective, some people disagree that any sort of ethnic separation ism including voluntary one only deepens ignorance and paves the way for prejudice. For them, it lessens the chance of informal social give and take that is needed for people ever really to get to know each other (peterI.Rose,penina M.Glazer,Myron glazer, 1978).

Hence, this argument holds the position that in a society two or more ethnic groups, conflict may arise. Roots of ethnic conflict can be political, economic, religious, linguistic cultural or racial. The reasons ethnic difference leads to conflict include (Kottak, 2002):

- A sense of injustice because of resource distribution
- Economic or political completion
- Prejudice
- Discrimination
- Hostility
- Unwillingness to interact
- Ethno centrism
- Ethnocide
- Forced assimilation
- Cultural colonialism
- Sharp Intolerance comes from the difference of language, skin color, religious beliefs ,customs and gender are among others (John and Erna perry, 1976; E.Conklin, 1987)

Finally, they conclude that domination, conflict and instability are inevitable features of plural societies. This is because each group considers its culture as superior over the other and any culture outside are inferior. Such kind of ethnocentrism leads to prejudice and discrimination, which are sufficient preconditions for conflict and violation. (Peter H.Dubline; Betty L.S. Bardige;Robert M.harrington;Jacqueline H.walsh, 1978:pp 289).But sume scholars observed that different ethnic groups can exist with out conflict when the groups occupy different ecological niches:they make their living in different ways and do not compete. Idealy they should depend on each other's activity and exchange with one another (Kottak C. p., 1994)

3.   How Multi Ethnicity Affect Development?

It is argued that for one reason or another, the existence of multi ethnic society direct affect on development of a nation, accommodates it. Whenever there are multiple ethnic groups, there exist a dominant group, which controls power and resource, and minority groups, which are subordinate to the dominant group. This arrangement facilitates the exploitation of minority groups would lead to revolutionary changes in a society as well as in our economy. If the conflict is un solvable through above mentioned mechanisms, final, the resource would be genocide: the killing off all members of the un wanted group. just a few examples (John and Erna perry, 1976: pp200-237).

- Of six million Jewish were murdered by Nazi Germany;
- of millions of life subjected to massacre in Bangladesh;
- of 200,000-500,000 Tutis were killed in Rwanda;
- more than 800,000 people have been displaced in Zaire;
- morthan14,000 have died in Sirilanka in clashes between Tamil and the Sinhalese;
- more than 130,000 have been killed in former Yugoslavia in 1991;
- up to 50,000 people were killed in Burundi in 1993 ;
- in Ethiopia,55,000 Tigrian youth sacrificed their life ;more than 100,000 suffered from physical damage ,2500 people of Hauzen city killed off air attack within single day in the struggle launched to end discrimination ,but this   data does   not   include   entire national human and material cost (Woldearegay, 2010)

In case minority groups prejudiced and discriminated, their ascribed status brings social, political, economic, and moral and employment marginalization. In this sense, discrimination and poverty are closely related, because the dominant group who controls power and strategic resource deprives the minority group access for theses resources. As result, ethnic minorities suffer all the disadvantages associated with this such as poor living conditions, wide unemployment   ,poor education and training, low social status, poor health condition, delinquency, low life expectancy, high divorce rate ,high rate of school dropouts, living in crowed dilapidated housing, in sufficient socio-political participation are all related to ethnic discrimination (E.Conklin, 1987:pp263).

Ethnic minorities not only suffer discrimination but also suffer from class, gender, and age inequalities as well. As it was noted in human history, discriminated minorities occupied mainly the bottom of the socio economic system, because of the nature of capitalism's class based colonial roots and postcolonial attitudes toward minority groups. The Rowan tee Foundation in 1995 claimed that ethnic minorities are more likely the fifth of the population and less likely than whites to be in the richest fifth are are. Women in ethnic minority are subject to dual oppression and confined to least privileged sections of the employment, suffering the effects of race, class and gender stereotypes (Mark Kirby and others, 1997).

In a nation characterized by the existence of ethnic inequality and discrimination, economic activities and social welfare suffer from instability and violence as those who lost their privilege, prestige and rights carry out revolution and collective action. Banding together in a collective action to change the way that dominant group treats them includes peaceful demonstration (protest) designed to reform the social structure through legal change and /or it can take violent disturbance form aimed at more basic alteration of the society. Success of such action requires human, economic and material cost would be spent for social and economic development. To mention single case example, in urban riot conducted in Miami in 1980,18 people dead and $80 million worth property was damaged (E.Conklin, 1987).The loss of life and property resulted from insurgency and revolution in less developed nations is incalculable and not studied yet.

4.   **Advantages and Disadvantages Of Assimilation And Multi Cultural Policies In Ethiopia Case**

Assimilation: forced assimilation: as Conklin(1987) states assimilation is sometimes forced on the minority group by dominating group that requires the minority group to abandon its language, traditions, and religion for those of dominant group. In fact, assimilation can be **voluntary**, occurring slowly over many years as ethnic group is observed in to the society at it s own pace. Voluntary assimilation is easiest if there are social, cultural, and physical similarity between the minority group and the dominant group.   Assimilation also takes the form of **acculturation**, a process by which a group adopts the dominant culture. This cultural integration can be encouraged through a system of public education that provides all groups with common cultural background and common language. **Amalgamation,** another form of assimilation occurs through marriage with other groups. **Structural assimilation** is a process by which people of different ethnic groups participate in both primary and secondary groups of larger society, including private clubs, community organizations, business and government (Gardon, 1964 cited in Conklin, 1987). In a structural assimilated society, people of all racial and ethnic backgrounds would have equal access to all positions, are represented in top positions in business, political parties, government and the mass media.

Assimilation policy tested so long in Ethiopia with the result of prolonged civil war and instability that hindered the social political and economic development. The policy initiated more than 17 struggle groups in Ethiopia and finally the struggle forces took over the power with new constitution allowing federal system for nations, nationalities and peoples of Ethiopia. Many agree, assimilation policy failed and it was the root cause for the loss of thousands of hundreds of Ethiopian from civil war, the formation of many nationalist rebellion groups and discrimination and social degradation (Woldearegay, 2010).

Pluralism: is a policy by which dominant groups allow minority groups to retain their cultural identity and the minority groups do not seek assimilation, a Varity of distinct groups co exist side by side in the same society. As Barth (1958/1968) defines plural society combining ethnic contrasts, ecological specialization and the economic independence of those groups. In plural society (Kottak C. P., 2002):

- Each group accommodates the other and tolerates cultural diversity
- Each group retains its own aspect of culture ,language ,religion, mode of dress, and religion holydays
- Group differences are not a source of negative discrimination
- No group suffer from a minority status
- No one group seeks to dominate other groups
- Intimate interaction and marriage usually continue to take place within each group to maintain its identity and to avoid assimilation in homogeneous society

As we can see points listed above, Pluralistic policy best works in multi cultural and multi ethnic society. Since each ethnic group naturally seeks freedom and maintaining its identity, as pluralism allows, pluralism is thought to be better solution to diminish inter-ethnic violation and discrimination. Pluralism better tested in Switzerland with better effect.

5.   Policy Recommendation to Ethiopian Government

Ethiopia is having multi ethnic societies with Varity of differences, which are potential for conflicts. Conflicts seen to be continue even federal system established after the downfall of Unitarian government. A study conducted in Addis Ababa University about the interaction of students from different Ethiopian ethnic background suggests   that Stereotypes, pejorative labeling and prejudice hurt feelings of a person or group and there by worsen ethnic tension in Ethiopia. The studies further show that ethnocentrism threatened the unity of students in Addis Ababa University (Hailemariam, 2010). This can be generalized in to entire Ethiopia society to see the extent of ethnocentrism in Ethiopia as potential danger for ethnic harmony.

some authorities also   maintain that   as a natural fact conflicts existed ,are existing and will continue to exist in Ethiopia ,however ,the way conflicts   should be alleviated would be democratic (Woldearegay, 2010).Conflicts of linguistic nature, land ownership ,religious have been common in current Ethiopia. Establishing federal system itself only does not bring sustained co existence and harmony. In addition, appropriate policy that addresses multi-ethnic interest, effective strategies to implement the policy and specific programs should be applied.

To sustain inter -ethnic - co existence, harmony and development in Ethiopia; I would suggest the following policy measures:

Maintain multi-cultural policy: multi-cultural policy views cultural diversity in a country as something desirable and to be encouraged .it appreciates the practice of many ethnic traditions and individuals in multi cultural society socialize not only in to dominant group(national) but also in to ethnic culture (Kottak C. P., 2002:pp 94)

Multi culturalism seeks ways for people to understand and inter act that donot depend on samness but on respect for differences.Multi-culturalism stresses the interaction of ethnic groups and their contribution to a country. It assumes that each group has something to offer and learn from others. Multiculturalism succeeds best in a society whose political system promotes freedom of expression and diverse ethnic groups (ibid).

Setting multi-cultural policy itself only does not bring sustained co existence and harmony. In addition, appropriate programs and action plans that address multi-ethnic interest, effective strategies to implement the policy and specific programs should be applied. Some strategies and programs are suggested bellow:

Pluralistic political system: the ideology of cultural pluralism is most widely accepted today. It stresses the desirability of each ethnic group's retaining its cultural distinctiveness rather than being assimilated in to the dominant culture (John and Erna perry, 1976 :pp 237). pluralism is a democratic political system(like belgium,netzerlandsand switzerlands)where the major ethnic groups share power through a coalition of their political leaders(Lijpart 1977 cited in Kottak C. P., 2002)

Affirmative action programs and affirmative action plans should be designed: affirmative action program is hiring policy designed to bring more women and minority group in to position s formerly closed to them. Affirmative action plans are one method of bringing minority groups in to areas from which they have been left out. To achieve real equality of opportunity Affirmative action programs and affirmative action plans should be set up . The idea of these programs and plans is that ,because past discrimination has left many members of minority groups without the skills for better jobs (Peter H.Dubline; Betty L.S. Bardige;Robert M.harrington;Jacqueline H.walsh, 1978 :pp204,289,300) .These programs to include:

- Giving minority group members a special edge when it comes to hiring and promoting
- Educational standards are relaxed ,and special training is given to help minority applicants get the job
- The minority workers are also given added support in getting new social settings
- Minority group members must be given increased opportunities

Reducing prejudice through specific programs and strategies

As multi cultural society, prejudice and discrimination are common attitudes in Ethiopian society too. They are potential danger for group coexistence and harmony. Hence, the following specific strategies are recommended (E.Conklin, 1987:pp 248,):

- Bringing the members of different groups in to direct contact through different events in equal and participatory manner
- Providing the opportunity for scientific and athletic completion between different groups Studies show that such completion in scientific activities such as literacy campaign, scientific exploration, agricultural production, sports contest seen to have reduce prejudice (J.Glossp, 1983 :pp 82).

- Fairly uniform system of education that maintains multiculturalism and national unity: Studies support the idea that uniform educational system inherited from French colony rule maintained national unity in certain countries despite ethnic contrast (Kottak C. P., 2002 :pp 56)
- Creating Active school system that involves co curricular activities ,research and events that promote core values help different ethnic groups to understand each other and common goals and issues (Hailemariam, 2010).
- Setting programs and activities that maintain national consensus between community ,political parties, institutions and classes(ibid)

Bibliography

E.Conklin, J. (1987). *Sociology:An introduction.* New york: Macmillan Pub.

Hailemariam, A. (2010, November). Ethnic Identy and the Relations of Amhara,Oromo and tigray students at Addis Ababa university Main Campus. *Anthology of peace a nd security Research .*

J.Glossp, R. (1983). *Confronting War.* Jefferson London: Mcfarland pub.

John and Erna perry. (1976). *The social web:An introduction to Sociology.* SanFransisco: Cuyahoga Community College.

Kottak, C. P. (2002). *Cultural Anthropology* (9 ed.). Boston: MacgrawHill.

Kottak, C. p. (1994). *Exploration of Human Diversity* (6 ed.). New york: The university of Michigan,Macgraw Hill Inc.

Mark Kirby and others. (1997). *Sociology in perispective .* Oxford blantyre: Heinemann Pub.

Peter H.Dubline; Betty L.S. Bardige;Robert M.harrington;Jacqueline H.walsh. (1978). *sociology:People in Groups.* Chicago: Science research inc.

peterI.Rose,penina M.Glazer,Myron glazer. (1978). *sociology :understanding Society.* New jersey: prentice-Hall INC. Engle Wood Cliffs.

Woldearegay, G. (2010). The Features of Struggle of National Equality. *Nations and Nationalities Day pannel Diacussion.* Mekele: MEkele University.